KEYED UP
A TUTOR FOR ELECTRONIC KEYBOARD

By Nancy Litten

Early Elementary (Pre-initial)

STUDENT EDITION

AlfredUK.com
keyboardcourses.com

First published in Great Britain in 2010
Copyright © MMX Alfred Publishing Co (UK) Ltd

Written by Nancy Litten

All rights reserved. Printed in the UK

EAN: 9780955544255
ISBN 0-9555442-5-4

Project producer Andrew Higgins
Cover by EBY Design Ltd
Engraving by Nancy Litten and Andrew Higgins
Music produced by Nancy Litten

KEYED UP
A TUTOR FOR ELECTRONIC KEYBOARD

Early Elementary (Pre-initial)

By Nancy Litten

It has been discovered that the main reason why students discontinue lessons is because of a lack of opportunity to play with others. It is assumed that if they are good at a skill they will enjoy it. Modern research has discovered that the reverse is more likely; if they enjoy something they will strive to become good at it.

This first tutor aims to address both those issues, providing material for group or individual tuition in the popular idiom, with suitably styled electronic keyboard accompaniments played by the teacher. The regular beat develops students' sense of pulse, and the interweaving teacher's melodies give students experience of ensemble, even in individual tuition. (It also makes the experience more enjoyable for the teacher!) The CD is of great benefit to teachers in the lesson, and to students in their practice; 'Sound before symbol' is today's maxim. Many of the ensembles are recorded twice, with and without the teacher's additional melody.

The teacher's book is in normal sized print and includes all the chords and contrasting melodies. The students' version (for Early-Elementary level only) is in large print and apart from pieces where they play the chords, contains their part only, in order to avoid confusion.

Tempi are given as a guide to final performance. Considerably slower speeds are advised at first. Initial, slow practice by students can be done just using the stated rhythmic groove as backing. Alternatively recordings stored on the keyboard or a memory device can be played back at altered tempi.

Notes covered in this book are C, D, E, F and G, with a new chapter incorporating each one. Note values encompass quarter notes (crotchets), half notes (minims) and whole notes (semibreves), including rests and some simple syncopation; time signatures are in simple time in quarter or half note beats. There is a minimum of written instruction; it is assumed that the teacher will elaborate.

In each chapter opportunities will be found for students to improvise to backings provided by the CD or the teacher; and to improve their grasp of notation by writing down their compositions. By the end of the book they will have encountered the left hand chords of C, G, F, Am and Dm, along with advice on how to improvise freely at home.

Nancy Litten

N.B. The terminology in this book is the same as that found in Trinity Guildhall publications. For example, the word 'voice' is used rather then 'tone'.

CONTENTS

TECHNIQUE 1 | See-Saw

The fingers are numbered 1 to 5, starting with the thumb. Rest the back of your hand on your knee
and relax the fingers. Then gently turn your hand over, keeping its rounded shape, and place it on the keyboard.
The thumb should be on C and the other fingers on the next notes, one over each.
See if you can alternate 1 and 5 smoothly and evenly like a well-balanced see-saw.

SOLOS

The pieces on the first two pages are all set to the same style and voice; they can be played individually
or as a continuous performance.

*N.B. The styles (but not the chords unless you are intended to play them) appear in the students' book,
as the rhythmic groove on its own can be a useful background when practising slowly.*

A One in Four Chance

 TRACK 1

This is the 'tempo'
↓

♩ = 95-115: Big Band Swing

Use the rhythmic backing of Big Band Swing for your practice and write in
the number or category. Use the sound setting of Pizzacato Strings and enter
the number or category for easy access.

Do this for each piece in the book.

4/4 = 4 crotchet beats in each bar

This piece begins with 4 bars rest

Look at the beginning
of the next line and
be ready to play

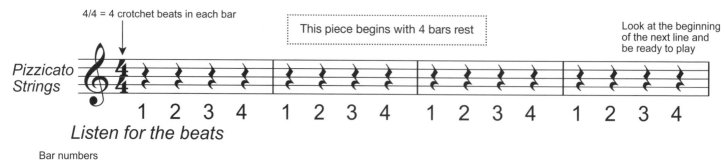

Listen for the beats

Bar numbers
↓

Start the next line

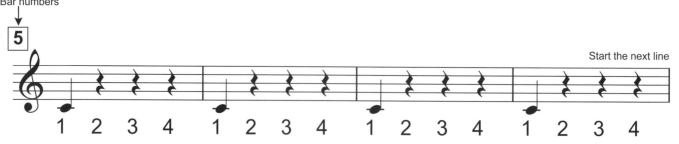

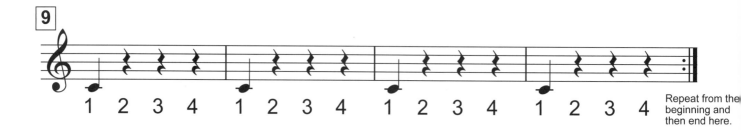

Repeat from the
beginning and
then end here.

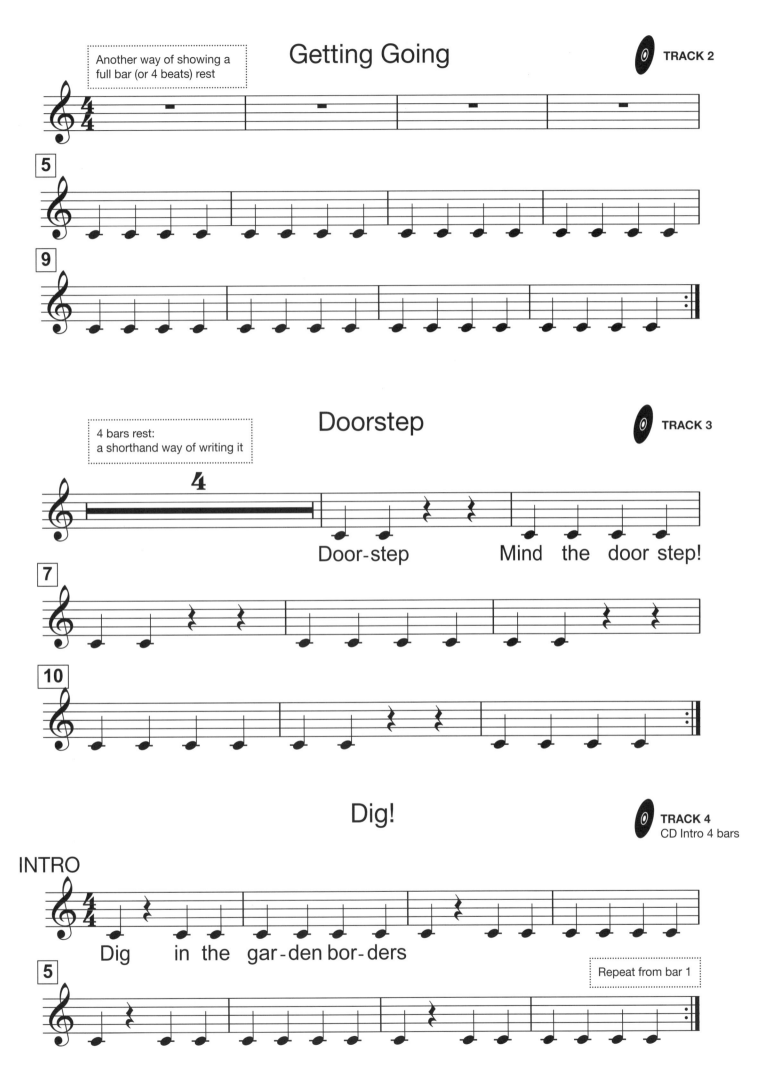

Hit Me With Your Rhythm Stick

 TRACK 5

This 1979 Number One hit by Ian Dury & The Blockheads was their most successful single.
It feastures one band member playing two saxophones at the same time!

Speak and/or play with an unpitched percussion sound on the keyboard.

♩ **= 165: Rock**

Dury & Jankel arr. Litten

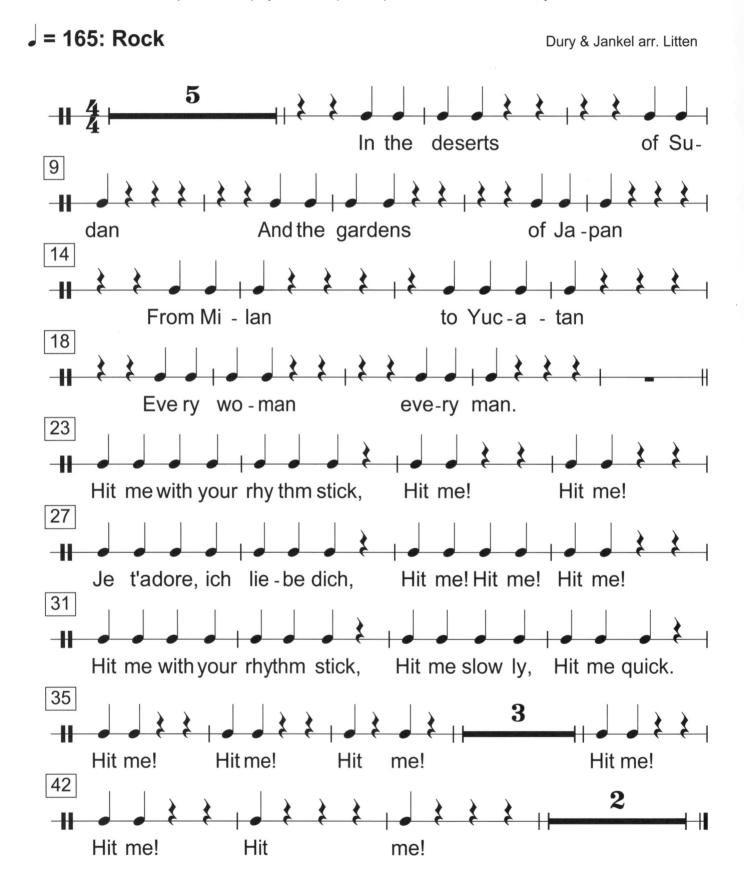

ENSEMBLES

He's Got The Whole World

TRACK 6/7
CD Intro 4 bars
including bar 1

♩ = **100: Rock 'n' Roll**

Trad. arr. Litten

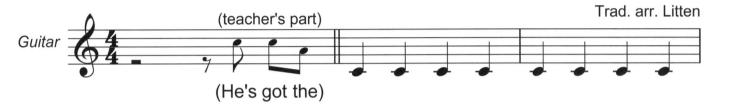

(teacher's part)

(He's got the)

Guitar

♩ Half-note (Minim)
= 2 Quarter-note (Crotchet) beats

▬ = half-note (Minim) rest

CHORD PRACTICE 1

Ten in the Bed

One chord throughout played by student

♩ = 120: Pop

Trad. arr Litten

C = chord symbol

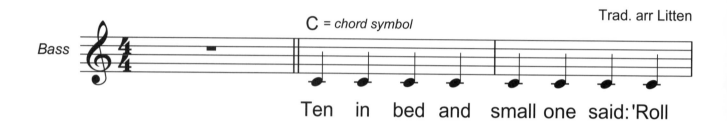

Ten in bed and small one said: 'Roll

o - ver, o - ver!' All rolled o - ver, one fell out, now

nine in bed and small one said 'Roll o - ver, o - ver!'
(seven)

All rolled o - ver, one fell out, now eight in bed and small one said 'Roll
(six)

o - ver, o - ver!' All rolled o - ver,

(Continue until no-one is left in bed!)

Shout!

 TRACK 8

*Marie Lawrie was discovered singing in Glasgow clubs with a local 'beat' group in 1962
when she was just 14. Their names were changed to Lulu and The Luvvers
and a year later they soared into the charts with this version of the 1959 Isley Brothers hit.*

♩ = **140: 60s Rock or 16 Beat Pop**

Isley, Isley and Isley arr. Litten

11

Cockles and Mussels

In Dublin you will find a statue of Molly Malone, said to be a
beautiful fishmonger who lived there in the 17th Century and died young.

PLAY YOUR OWN! WRITE YOUR OWN! 1

Listen to the CD or ask your teacher to play the auto-accompaniment, and make up a melody with the notes you have used in this chapter. Ask your teacher to help you to write it down. Choose your own voice, and give the piece a title when completed.

Notes: **C**

Note Values: ♩ = 1 beat   ♩ = 2 beats   ♩. = 3 beats   𝅝 = 4 beats

              (...and don't forget to include some rests!)

Title: ....

Voice: ....

TRACK 11
CD Intro 4 bars

N.B. The chords of the accompaniment are shown here, not for you to play, but to indicate the harmonies over which you are improvising

♩ = 95: Pop

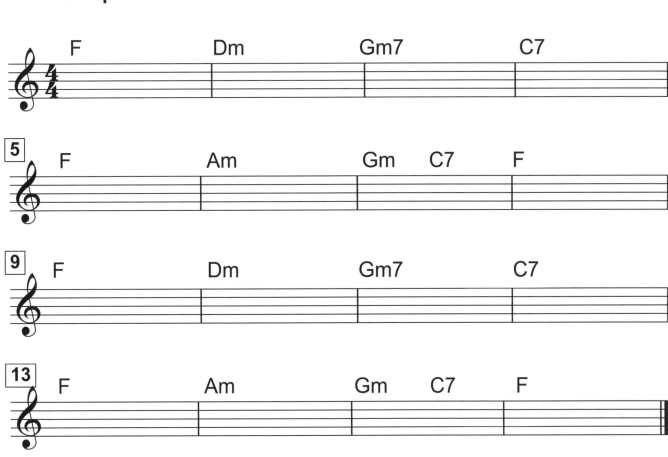

ENSEMBLES

Walzing Matilda

TRACK 12/13
CD Intro 4 bars

*A famous 1895 'bush ballad', it has almost become Australia's unofficial
national anthem. It tells of a man who has stolen a sheep
and put it in his 'matilda' (swag bag).*

♩ = 86: Bluegrass

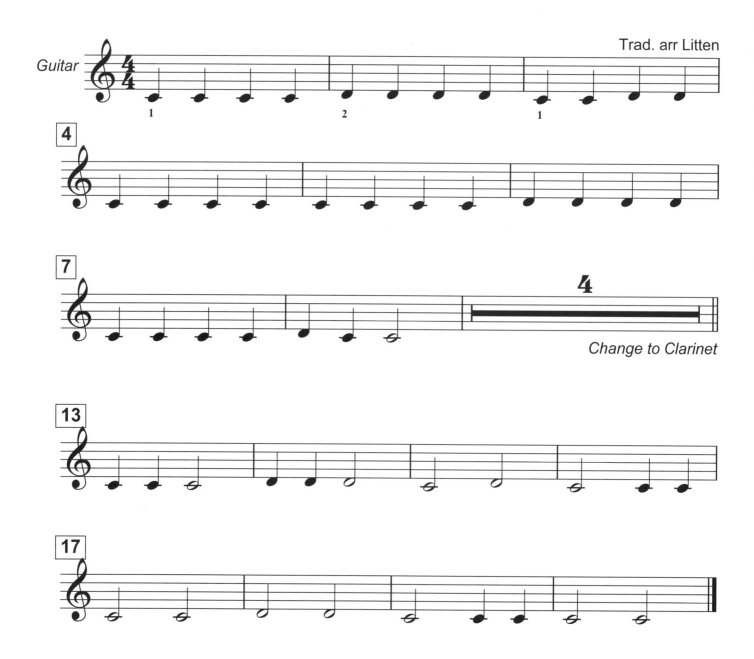

Go, Tell It On The Mountain

TRACK 14/15
CD Intro 4 bars

An African-American spiritual dating from about 1865.

♩ = 95: Country

Rule Britannia!

This song was part of a 'masque' (musical play) written for George II.
The words (by Scottish poet James Thomson) celebrated British pride in people being allowed
more freedoms than other nations, and were set to music by Thomas Ame. It soon developed a life of it's
own, and, when heard in London in 1745, became an instant hit.

Return To Sender

TRACK 18
CD Intro 2 bars

*This song was a Number One hit for Elvis Presley in 1962.
It is about a man mailing a letter to his girlfriend after a tiff. She keeps sending it back to him
unopened with the following reasons written on the envelope.*

♩ = 120: Rock 'n' Roll

Scott and Blackwell arr Litten

(Return to sender)   Add-ress un-known,

No such num-ber   No such zone.

(play an octave higher)

TECHNIQUE 2 | Legato

See how smoothly you can move from note to note. (Chords played by the teacher)

♩ = 100: Ballad

C & D SOLOS

The backings can be played on the CD or by the teacher. (The teacher could possibly play the melody in a contrasting voice.) Intros are the on-board keyboard ones for the style unless written out, as in this first one.

Dinner Dance

TRACK 19

♩ = 100: Jazz

That's The Way I Like It

 TRACK 23

*Released in 1975 by KC and the Sunshine Band, it became their second Number One hit,
and is widely considered the most popular song of the disco era.*

If there is more than one student; share out the notes marked out in brackets

© 1975 EMI Longitude. Faber Music Ltd.

Go back to the sign at bar 9
and play as far as the Fine bar.

CHORD PRACTICE 2 | C & G (I & V)

> N.B. You may need to lower the volume of the accompaniment because the Marimba is a quiet voice

Sambarimba

Chords played by student

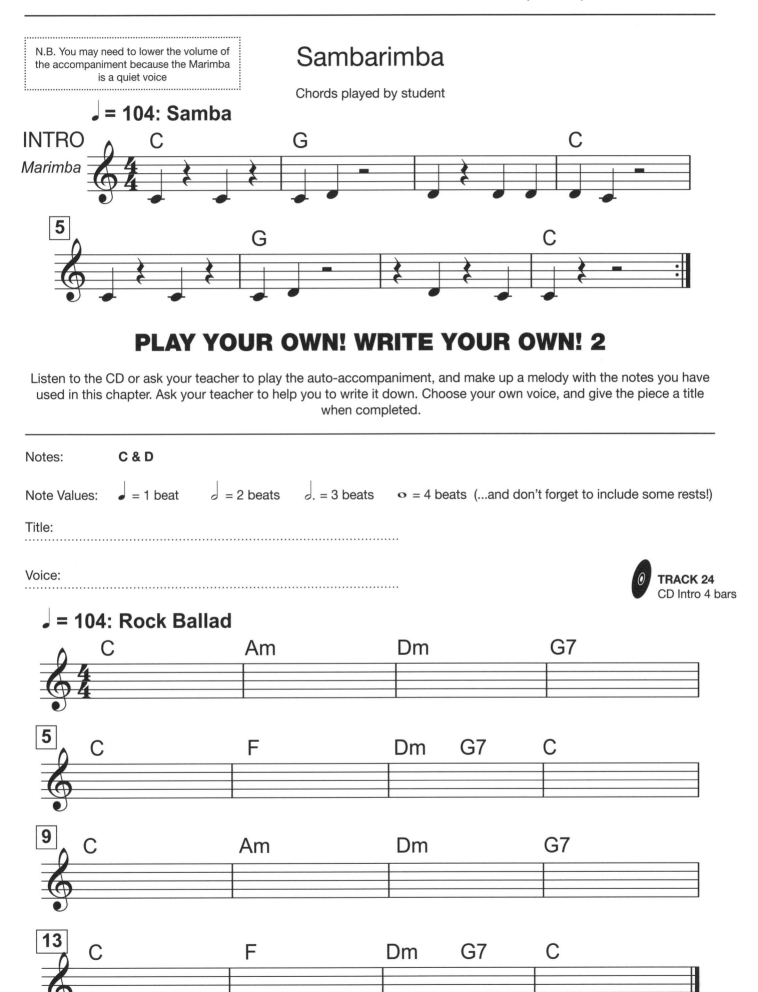

PLAY YOUR OWN! WRITE YOUR OWN! 2

Listen to the CD or ask your teacher to play the auto-accompaniment, and make up a melody with the notes you have used in this chapter. Ask your teacher to help you to write it down. Choose your own voice, and give the piece a title when completed.

Notes: **C & D**

Note Values: ♩ = 1 beat   ♩ = 2 beats   ♩. = 3 beats   𝅝 = 4 beats (...and don't forget to include some rests!)

Title:
....

Voice:
....

TRACK 24
CD Intro 4 bars

ENSEMBLES

My Bonnie

A traditional Scottish folk song; it may refer to 'Bonnie Prince Charlie', the Young Pretender to the British throne in the 18th Century.

♩ = 120: Waltz

Don't Sit Under The Apple Tree

The best-known song from this trio of songwriters, it has been a hit for many singers and bands since it was written in 1942. 'Don't sit under the apple tree with anyone else but me...til I come marching home'.

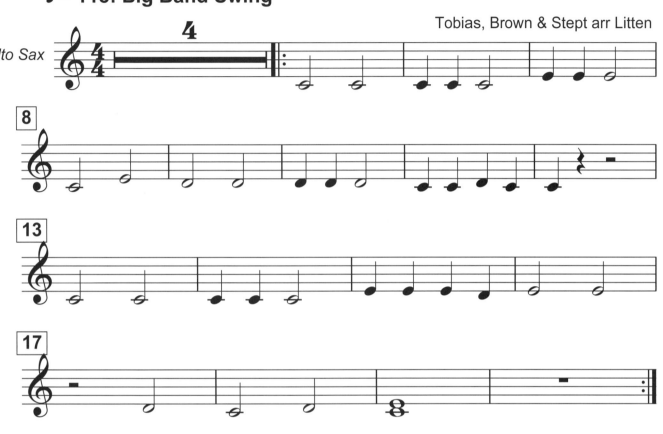

Tobias, Brown & Stept arr Litten

TECHNIQUE 3 | Slur it!

Slur It!

Chords played by student.
Make sure that the final crotchet in each bar is short.

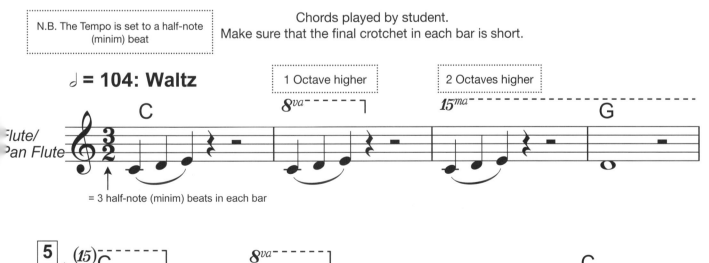

C, D & E SOLOS

The backings can be played on the CD or by the teacher. (The teacher could possibly play the melody in a contrasting voice.) Intros are the on-board keyboard ones for the style.

Autumn Sunrise

TRACK 28
CD Intro 4 b

♩ = 85: Rock Ballad

Remembering

TRACK 29
CD Intro 4 ba

♩ = 85: 8-Beat Ballad

24

In The Bar

♩ = 85: Big Band Swing

Wide Awake

♩ = 95: Pop

Ballad Of The Prairies

♩ = 95: Country Ballad

The Dance Floor

♩ = 95: Jazz Ballad

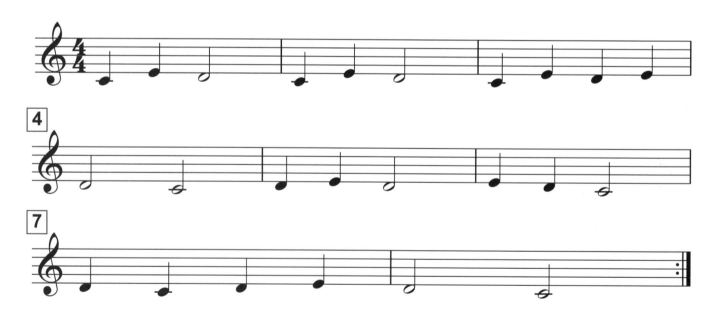

ENSEMBLES

Carefree Song

 TRACK 34/35

(New Note F)

Greensleeves

TRACK 36/37
CD Intro 4 bars
including bar 1

The 16th Century 'Dittye of the Lady Greene Sleeves'
was already well-known by the time of Shakespeare who mentions it in his 1602 play
'The Merry Wives of Windsor'; 'Let the sky rain potatoes! Let it thunder to the tune of 'Greensleeves!'

♩. = 40: 6/8 Ballad, or

♩ = 120: Waltz

Trad. arr Litten

28

Little Chapel On The Prairie

♩ = 100: Country Waltz   Chords played by student

'Tied' note: hold for 6 beats

PLAY YOUR OWN! WRITE YOUR OWN! 3

Listen to the CD or ask your teacher to play the auto-accompaniment, and make up a melody with the notes you have used in this chapter. Ask your teacher to help you to write it down. Choose your own voice, and give the piece a title when completed.

Notes: **C, D & E**

Note Values: ♩ = 1 beat   ♩ = 2 beats   ♩. = 3 beats   o = 4 beats   (...and don't forget to include some rests!)

Title: ....   Voice: ....

♩ = 78: Ballad

TRACK 38
CD Intro 4 bars

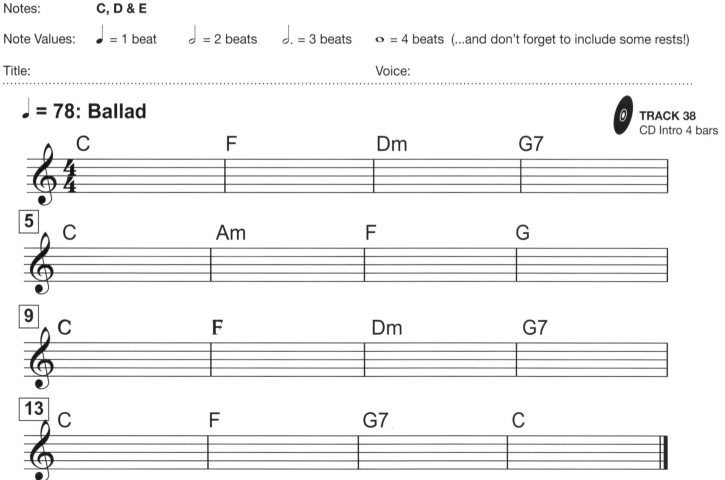

ENSEMBLES

Drunken Sailor

A famous sea-shanty, first published in the 1820s.
The chorus asks "What shall we do with a drunken sailor?"
and the verses suggest increasingly vigorous ways of sobering him up!

♩ = 60: Polka

Trad. arr. Litten

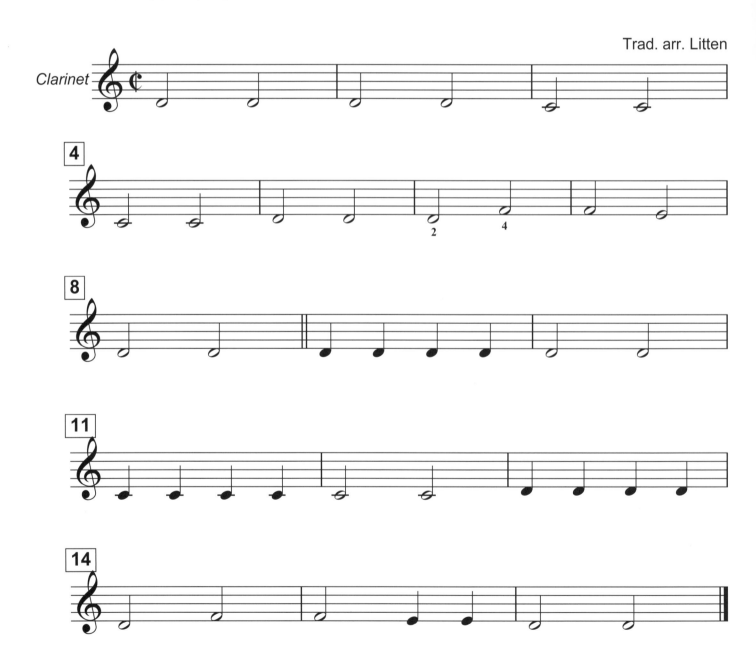

We Will Rock You

TRACK 40

A '7-inch' single was released by the rock band Queen in 1977 with 'We Will Rock You' on one side,
and 'We Are The Champions' on the other; as they are often sung together.
The 'stomp, stomp, clap' backing is said to have been inspired by farm machinery.

♩ = c.140:

May arr. Litten

Clap

Foot stamps

5

Overdrive Guitar

We   will,   we   will   rock   you

9

Clap

Foot stamps

13

17

Overdrive Guitar

We   will,   we   will   rock   you

21

We   will,   we   will   rock   you   *Stamp!*

John Brown's Baby

*'John Brown's Body', or 'Battle Hymn of the Rupublic', was a union marching song from the
American Civil War (1861-1865) using a tune from the earlier settler days.
Here it is given a humorous twist as the song of a parent massaging a child's chest with
camphorated oil to relieve the symptoms of a cold, and making a game of it.*

♩ = 90: March

Trad. arr. Litten

32

33 *...more rests than notes!*

4. John Brown's got on

35 John Brown's got on

37 John Brown's got on so

39 rub with cam - phor oil!

41 **Chorus**

Cam - phor - a - ted,

43 Cam - phor - a - ted,

45 Cam - phor - a - ted,

47 rub with oil!

C, D, E & F SOLOS

The backings can be played on the CD or by the teacher. (The teacher could possibly play the melody in a contrasting voice.) Intros are the on-board keyboard ones for the style.

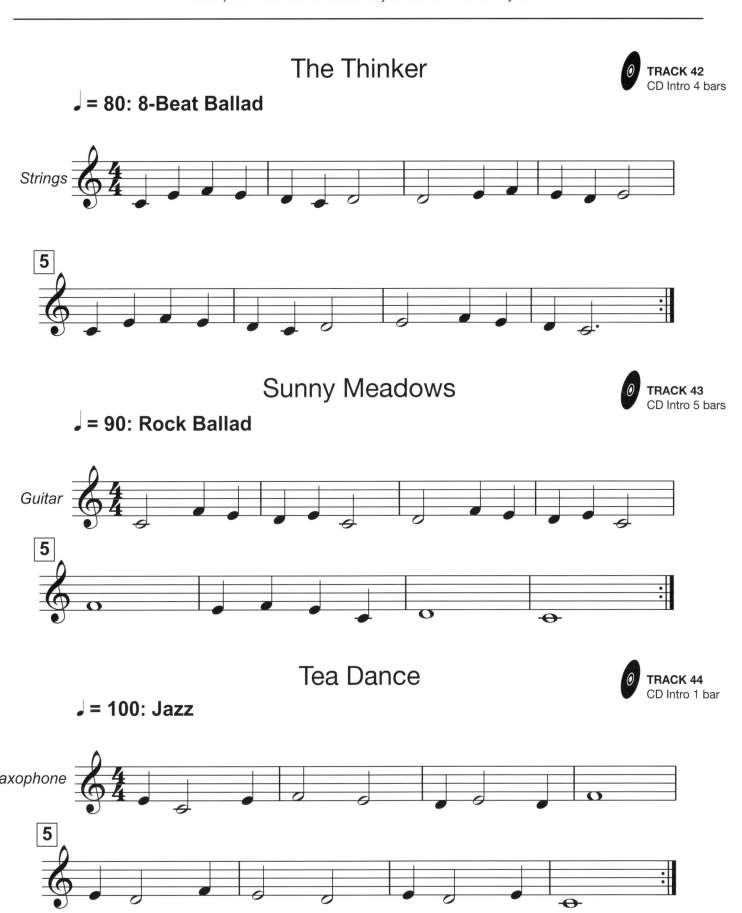

The Thinker

TRACK 42
CD Intro 4 bars

♩ = 80: 8-Beat Ballad

Strings

Sunny Meadows

TRACK 43
CD Intro 5 bars

♩ = 90: Rock Ballad

Guitar

Tea Dance

TRACK 44
CD Intro 1 bar

♩ = 100: Jazz

Saxophone

Song Of Travel

TRACK 45
CD Intro 4 b

♩ = 100: Techno

Happy Memories

TRACK 46
CD Intro 4 ba

♩ = 95: Ballad

ENSEMBLES

Swing Low

TRACK 47/48
CD Intro 4 bars

Swing Low was composed by Wallis Willis, a freed slave, in the 1860s.
He lived in the Indian Territory of Choctow, Oklahoma, where the Red River
reminded him of the River Jordan and the story of the Prophet Eijah being taken to heaven by a chariot.

♩ = 80: Soul

37

A Spoonful Of Sugar

Julie Andrews sings this song as the magical governess 'Mary Poppins'
in the 1964 Disney film, encouraging the two children in her charge to tidy their room.

♩ = 135: Foxtrot (not swung)

🄐 = A 'Pause': Hold these notes a little longer

Sherman & Sherman arr . Litten

© 1964 Warner/Chappell. Faber Music Ltd.

TECHNIQUE 4 | Dexterity

Chords played by student

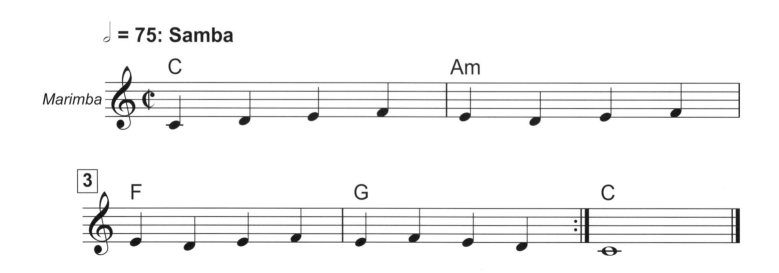

♩ = 75: Samba

CHORD PRACTICE 4

One Man Went To Mow

This tune needs only two chords, C and G (I & V), but it introduces
Chapter 5's new note G. Make some of the notes dotted if you wish.

♩ = 105: Country Swing   Chords played by student

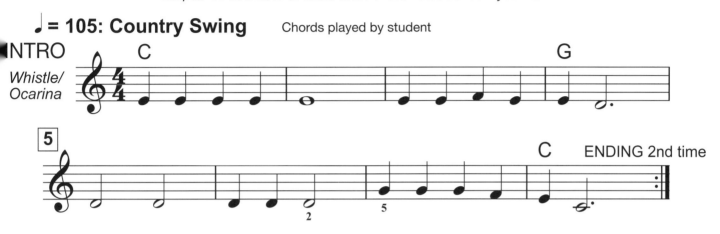

PLAY YOUR OWN! WRITE YOUR OWN! 4

Listen to the CD or ask your teacher to play the auto-accompaniment, and make up a melody with the notes you have used in this chapter. Ask your teacher to help you to write it down. Choose your own voice, and give the piece a title when completed.

Notes: **C, D, E & F**

Note Values: ♩ = 1 beat   ♩ = 2 beats   ♩. = 3 beats   o = 4 beats (...and don't forget to include some rests!)

Title: Voice:
....

♩ = 100: 8-Beat

TRACK 51
CD Intro 4 bars

ENSEMBLE

Uprising

 TRACK 52

Lead vocalist and guitarist of the progressive rock band Muse, Matthew Bellamy, wrote this song.
It was released as the lead single from their fifth album 'The Resistance' in 2009.

♩ = 130: Rock Shuffle

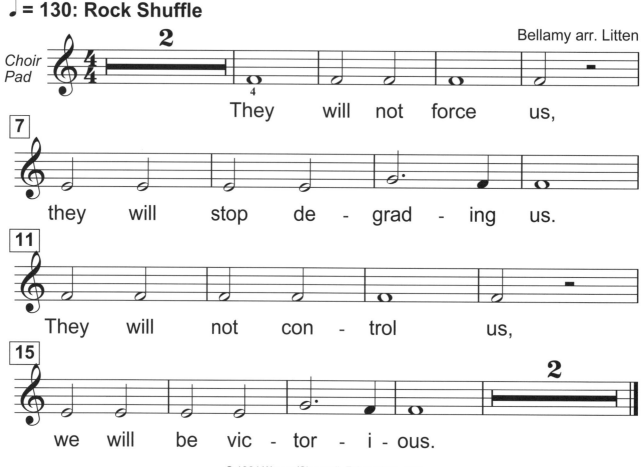

© 1964 Warner/Chappell. Faber Music Ltd.

TECHNIQUE 5 | Walking the Dog

Chords played by student

♩ = 100: Bluegrass

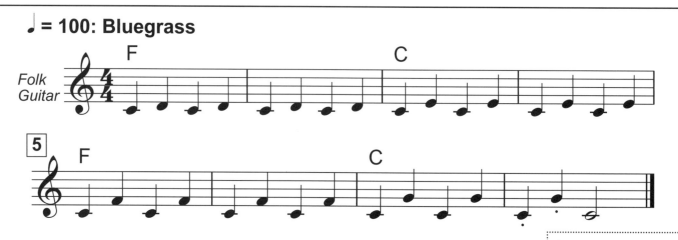

Short notes 'staccato'

ENSEMBLE

The Lavender Coloured Horse

TRACK 53/54
CD Intro 4 bars

Chords played by student

♩ = 110: Jazz Waltz

N.B. You may need to lower the volume of
the accompaniment because the Marimba
is a quiet voice

C, D, E, F & G SOLOS

The backings can be played on the CD or by the teacher. (The teacher could possibly play the melody in a contrasting voice.) Enterprising students might be able to accompany themselves in Margate Sands, Motorway, and Dancing Shoes as the chords are known. Intros are the on-board keyboard ones for the style. Work up to a speed of quarter-note (crotchet) = 100 on each piece.

Margate Sands

♩ = 100: Disco

TRACK 55
CD Intro 4 bars

Motorway Drive

♩ = 100: Hip-Hop

TRACK 56
CD Intro 4 bars

Chill-Out Music

♩ = 100: 8-Beat Standard

TRACK 57
CD Intro 4 bars

Open Country

TRACK 58
CD Intro 1 bar

♩ = 100: Rock Ballad

At Home On The Ranch

TRACK 59
CD Intro 9 bars

♩ = 100: Country Rock

Dancing Shoes

♩ = 100: **Dance Pop**

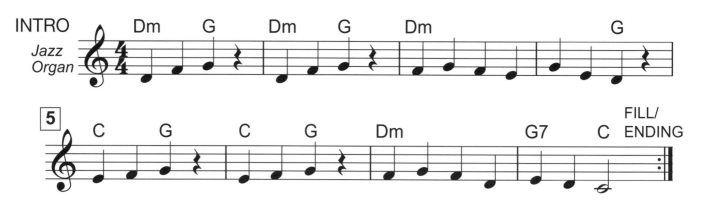

Dance Band Solo

♩ = 100: **Dixieland**

ENSEMBLES

Men Of Harlech

TRACK 62/63
CD Intro 4 bars
including bar 1

This Welsh folk tune was given lyrics in the late 19th Century.
They commemorate the siege of Harlech castle between 1461 and 1468,
the longest in British history.

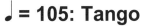 **= 105: Tango**

N.B. Students enter during the last bar of the Intro

Trad. arr . Litten

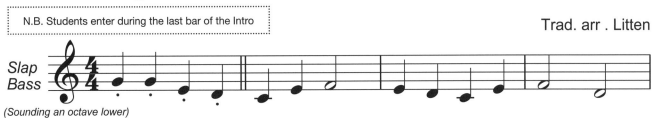

Slap Bass
(Sounding an octave lower)

The Jazzy Duke

♩ = 105: Boogie

No Woman No Cry

 TRACK 66

This reggae song was performed by Bob Marley and The Wailers in 1974.
It mentions Trenchtown - a ghetto of Kingston, Jamaica.
From the royalties, Marley's friend Vincent Ford was able to fund a soup kitchen there.

Chords played by student
If wished the Am chords can be Am7

♩ = 80: **Reggae**

Ford arr Litten

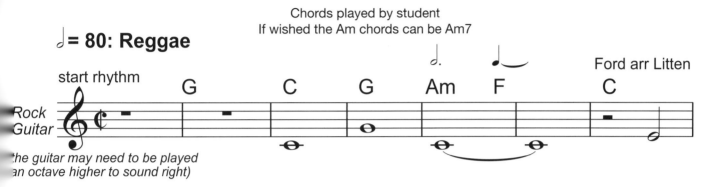

(the guitar may need to be played
an octave higher to sound right)

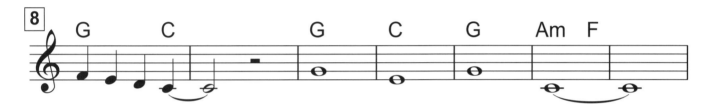

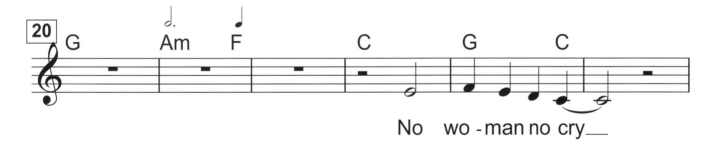

No wo-man no cry___

FIRST CONCERT PIECE

The student part can be played as a solo, or a duet with the teacher's added descant.

Sunshine Through The Leaves

TRACK 67/68
CD Intro 4 bars

♩ = 95: **Ballad**   Chords played by student

Jingle Bells

TRADITIONAL
arr. A.L.Christopherson

Jingle bells, jingle bells,
Jingle all the way,
Oh what fun it is to ride
In a one-horse open sleigh. Oh!
Jingle bells, jingle bells,
Jingle all the way,
Oh what fun it is to ride
In a one-horse open sleigh.

CHORD PRACTICE 5 | Improvising

1. Find a slow Ballad at tempo 60 and a voice such as Choir. Ask you teacher to play alternate bars of Dm and Am while you improvise on the notes C D & E, even adding G later (but not F). Then try it by yourself, with both hands. (If wished Am7 and Dm7 could be used.) In ending you could 'fade out', using the VOLUME CONTROL.

2. This can be played entirely on your own. Use a Country style at tempo 60 and a Guitar voice. Alternate one bar of C and one of F while you improvise in the right hand. Start with just notes C and D, and gradually add E and G as you become more confident. End finally on chord C. Don't forget to include rests in your melodies.

PLAY YOUR OWN! WRITE YOUR OWN! 5

Listen to the CD or ask your teacher to play the auto-accompaniment (or try playing it yourself!) and make up a melody with the notes you have used in this chapter. Ask your teacher to help you to write it down. Choose your own voice, and give the piece a title when completed.

Notes: **C, D, E, F & G**

Note Values: ♩ = 1 beat   ♩ = 2 beats   ♩. = 3 beats   o = 4 beats   (...and don't forget to include some rests!)

Title: ....

Voice: ....

♩ = 100: Waltz

TRACK 69
CD Intro 5 bars

NOW YOU ARE READY FOR **KEYED UP: Elementary!**

INDEX

Songs in alphabetical order